Two Train Town

poems by

Theresa Burns

Finishing Line Press
Georgetown, Kentucky

Two Train Town

Publisher: Leah Maines
Editor: Christen Kincaid
Cover Art: *South Orange Rush*, Joy Yagid
Author Photo: Joy Yagid
Cover Design: Glenn Wright

Printed in the USA on acid-free paper.
Order online: www.finishinglinepress.com
             also available on amazon.com

Author inquiries and mail orders:
Finishing Line Press
P. O. Box 1626
Georgetown, Kentucky 40324
U. S. A.

Contents

for Evan and Marie and Gregory

LITTLE FLOWER IN JERSEY

the children: having left to take the standardized tests at school,
   relieved to escape my anxiety, flashcards—

     the name: did they call me Avila or Lisieux, woman or child?
  did I crave my inheritance?

       the body: I won't die young like she did. I won't shower
this morning, since later I'll swim, fatherless—

the history: sister upon sister, order only when no one is home, echo of
   bathrooms—

     the husband: calls from jury duty, makes his way from courthouse
      to Newark Broad, goes mute—

     the hands: ordinary, which is to say sacred. they link, inexorably,
  to celebrity news. watch over me—

the apparition: she is painting the rooms again, this time more white.
              a girl reclines on grass, throws her head back—

TWO TRAIN TOWN

Because the teenagers wear their hair
a little long some in cornrows

and roam the streets in pairs
and wait outside friends' doors
in arcs of lamplight

idling on the porch.
Because we didn't need a car.

Because the trains travel at two angles
to one point in the city,
and the city broke our hearts.

We watched them on a weekday morning
restoring the brick
firehouse, fortifying the towers.

Because the old people live
in stylish buildings, ambulances
idling cheerfully out front.

Because they fixed the broken windows.
Fixed our broken.

When we first came it was summer,
but we imagined the hill in snow,
the kids on colorful sleds—

    you could see it from either train—

and all the colorful gloves left there
the next day.

BRICK CITY

Sorry, did I brush you?
Did I touch the soft

meadowland
above your elbow

by mistake?
Did I stroke you

on the train as I leaned
for what I needed?

Did I break you,
did it send us to our corners

into pieces, did I
knife you while the night outside

turned black the window,
turned our faces inside out?

Unbearable this nearness,
can you face me,

this approximation
of kinship, do you hate me,

to our corners you can
switch here, Brick City,

sorry, get hitched
here, sorry. Erase this

strangeness was there something
I missed here sorry

did I break you
by mistake?

FORECLOSURE SONNET

Already the coral bells, *heuchera*, 'caramel'
and 'lime rickey,' the azalea's olive head,
already the lamb's ear rising, half-mast from its pool
of dead leaves. Before a single robin,
the earth splits open, and shy teenagers appear
in their shorts and tanks, oh we must
avert our eyes from so much beauty,
the oak leaf spooling back its brittle skin
another year, a walk among the ghostly fronds,
our boots sodden, the clay-earth of the Oranges
warms and softens and sucks. Already the ivy
along Laura's porch greens, though she is
not coming back, and we, skeptics, late
blooms, against our propped-up dreams, still here.

THE GILDED AGE

Before I got to watch the American goldfinch
flash through the branches of the Leyland cypress this morning,

then fly off, leaving me slack jawed, prayerful—
I had to descend the scary staircase to our basement,

trip on the mops, brooms, baskets of old hats,
old gloves, to drain the sludge from the boiler,

catch that muck in the ancient, mud-
splattered bucket under the slop sink, strain to read

through the sight glass the water line as it
bobbed and bobbed, then met its match. I was alone,

so allowed myself the indulgence of comparison
with medieval toilers, a wet nurse hauling pails of boiling

water amid the wails and orders of my mistress, a servant
emptying chamber pots into the street. Before this,

I had to sift the stack of papers here at the table
that threaten to snuff me—bills, parking tickets, permission

slips, stuff I'm supposed to read, homework
I'm supposed to sign, her social studies report—

which is the reason I even know
what an American goldfinch looks like, the striking black strip

of its crown, how it dangles upside down from America's
back yard, that its nest is woven so tight it can hold water.

WHY I HATE MOM

I can't open the file
my son has left
on the desktop: *Why I Hate Mom.*

Just as well.
Why give him one more
item to list?

Unlikely I could decode
any of its secrets. Already his brain hums
ten times as fast.

He holds
so many cloaks
before me, folds them away
as I approach.

Does he mention the essay
I had him write? What he truly wants
from this life—

five paragraphs
of goals and refinements, a punishment
for some failing,
abandonment of purpose.

Give some examples, I said.
Maybe a nice
illustration or two.

I won't—and this
was the genius part—
even look at it,
I promised.
It's entirely for you.

So write
how you *really* feel.
And have fun with it.

LEARNING TO WRITE

In spite of the house.
In spite of the furnace of his attention,
I could not warm up.

So bottled-up, bottle-
necked, you could have stuck
a candle in my throat.
And he, same brown shoes, same size—

In the next room, in shrinking pajamas,
in wet bathing suits,

our children
frictioned and lit. All day

it went like this.
By the time I wiped the counter
after breakfast,

they'd shape-shifted again.

Before I started the engine,
they were deep in the caves

of their language making, in Lascaux,
in Canyon de Chelly.
They were the Anasazi bearing pencils

like shards, dye of vegetable,
crushed berry, spit—

I could hardly bear
to witness it. Chicken scratches, stick figures
trembled from dubious grips,

and the whole place littered with bits of paper
as they built their fires.

AFTER HER 47-YEAR-OLD-BROTHER DIED

Virginia came over
Most Tuesdays
To make a ratatouille
From a tattered book.

She brought vegetables
From the farm coop,
Chopped and measured
While she talked.

Eggplant, zucchini,
Bell pepper and onion.
Sometimes she teared up
When she breathed

Under the lid.
Or brought up the three girls
He left behind: *I still
Can't believe*, she'd say,

Moving on to froth
The insides of a pumpkin pie,
That it happened.
I poured more wine.

Occasionally, while she
Deveined the celery,
Or smashed whole
Cloves of garlic

With the heel of her hand,
Her phone
Would ping: the wife
Again texting, *Where are you?*

THE PLAY

The lawn was hacked up
like hamburger meat when we finished.
We were seven, nine, and eleven.
He was sixteen and so cool
we called him The Rock—
he shimmered at us
from an island of cool.
He gave us the play in his open hand,
his finger running along the lines
where he wanted us to run. It stopped
when he wanted us to stop, where
he felt he could get us the ball.
We knew nothing about the game
but what my brother taught us
those few Saturdays before
girlfriends, college: To go out
maybe five fast strides,
and at the right moment,
the place he'd shown us in his hand,
to turn to him; that is, fake,
then run hard in the other direction,
while our man fell in dirt
trying to follow. Then to catch
the floating bullet from him,
cradle it in our arms,
which we almost never did,
receive, that is.

ODE TO A CAR

I was never more grateful, you graceful
Passat wagon, with two-toned leather seats
and sick sound system we bought
in flusher times, than the day you broke down
when it was our turn to carpool,
and I had to ask the other kids' mother
if I could take her car to school,
and it would have to be that mother who is never
undone, who runs the impeccable
cookie drive, the mid-winter Blues Buster
with perfect gusto, who descended her staircase
at 7 am, a little surprised in her bathrobe, but tossed me
the keys to her minivan, which I had a little trouble
starting, but was soon humming down the block,
children resettled in the back, not apologizing
to them, not even turning to see the inscrutable
faces my kids wore that year we lived
below the poverty line, and every action
or inaction seen through that lens, that side mirror
that followed us to school and back, to Macy's,
the dentist and the deli counter, not caring
to hash out why they weren't getting braces
or a drink with that. They got to class
just five minutes late, and the fix for once
was quick and cheap, and you bet I stopped at the carwash
after, had you sudsed and buffed
to your former brilliance, even springing
for the undercarriage wax and sealant, so that
next morning when those girls slid in your indigo
doors, their mother would forget the image
of me in their driveway, unable
to remove the key from her ignition,
asking her to please come down a second time
to help.

KNIGHTS OF COLUMBUS

When my father totaled the white Volvo
leaving his own driveway,
the airbag bloomed
like a calla lily, sparing him
the stares of the gathering neighbors. The sky
was just turning apricot. A downy tapping
on the hide of a dogwood.

He came out to find my mother, he told us.
She could have gone wandering
again, knocking on
strangers' doors without her teeth,
though she hadn't walked
the length of the block in years.

Maybe they quarreled. Maybe he
threatened something and left,
and in the middle of it, forgot what he'd say
if he got there.
He woke with a scratch on his chin.

Let him think what he thinks, we know
why it happened.
The dinner in his honor that night. Monsignor himself
would make the toast. O Grand Knight!
O steadfast heart! They would bestow the purple raiment, heap
unbearable praise on him.

PROPORTION

When I say that his black
               leather belt gleamed
through the loops on his hips—

Are you thinking
that he used it on us?

He didn't.
On his six four frame
it held up his pants,

which grew looser
as he aged,
               the belt traveling

higher on the gut, almost
comical, a Stanley

and an Ollie of a father.
Even as he shrank, the belt
rose, kept pace.

               But on those
few occasions we came home

late, shoeless,
having played so long
on our dull block,

        our feet filthy, numb—

Did he hit us on the high
back of the head,

knock the hair
into our eyes, snap us
                aware of those

twilight dangers? Who remembers.

And if he did, it struck us
as nothing uncalled for,
            entirely in proportion

to the act—
            our forcing him to notice
what we almost
got away with.

I FIGHT WITH MARIE, WHO IS FIVE

Looking out the bedroom window after a morning of hard rain,
the wind drying off the streets, the driveway, like some enormous, God-
held blow dryer, I have to admire the neighbors' lawns, the shrubbery
blown clean the day before by laborers with oversized machines.
Even the row of white pines they planted
across the street when they took the copper beech down—
the hundred-and-fifty-year-old tree
sawed down, branch by elephant-hided branch,
over nine hours, while the people next door wept,
and someone actually called the police—
look particularly green and supple
in this late November light. *Sometimes I need to be right*, she said.
And she's right. Then we sat down like a country
finally at peace: war torn, philosophical.

COMMUNITY GARDEN

Did you mean to leave this onion for me?
Was it hiding in your bed last season? Neighbor,
what is bunched and greening in the plot
that's mine this year: your labor.

The cilantro that didn't make it
to your table, overwintered. I lifted it,
lay it like a fainted girl on the counter by my sink,
where I forgot it, I'm afraid. Now it's

drowned and yellowed,
not even fit to sniff. But the parsley I saved
—thank you. I dug it up with gloved hands
on a cold Saturday and cleaned it.

That very night I steamed a piece of delicate
fish and savored it, a curlicue of lemon at my wrist.

EDEN

We have not even entered the gourmet
grocery store, five o'clock, a time when everyone else
has the same idea, the parking lot
a teeming metropolis, requiring strategies
and decisions I am not capable of
these weeks since you died, and already
they are fighting. I choose to blame
her this time. My arm finds its way
around his shoulder; we pull a step ahead. And when, an hour later,
we leave the whooshing doors, the smell of teriyaki chicken
almost overwhelming, in my bag the reddest strawberries
I've ever seen, she turns and asks,
Am I being good today? my first thought
is not what you might have said, or done, but how odd
the question sounds, so bold and unattached
to anything, a question I would have
wanted you to answer, yes, but never asked.

RAINY DAY WOMEN

How gently we spoke with each other
the first weeks after he died.
At the house, huddled in his bed together,
and later on the phone, when we returned to our
other families. Each weekend in April:
rain and more rain. Gently we brought her
the photos, helped her glue and press
their bodies close again. She in his uniform and army cap,
she holding his black dog. And when our names
no longer came to her but mixed
like the names of the first weak flowers in the yard,
when the filters were finally shot, she looked up
from her work. *There's just one thing I don't understand. How
did I get so damn good looking?*

MARRIAGE ENCOUNTER

So indifferent did I take that kiss you gave him
each morning, and the one, identical,
when he returned each evening, lasting only a parched second,
that I didn't at first comprehend
the words in the notebook I found in your closet
from that weekend. But I read them.
And when it became clear, when I understood
that I shouldn't, read them faster.
The question: What do you love about him?
and your answer, which went on for six pages,
made my throat dry, my heart knock around in my chest
like a pinball slowly pulled back and let fly.
After ten minutes I was too dizzy to continue.
And it's true—when I stumbled
downstairs, a different woman worked the stove
in the dust-filled light, making the casserole we liked,
and the blood pulsing through the hand
that rested on your waist was different,
and your waist
was different, your hair,
the man hurrying from the train station
on his elegant legs, a different man.

IN MANHATTAN, WE DON'T MEET FOR LUNCH

Even when I'm not aware
I'm getting close to you,
say, my 34th to your 16th,

the sidewalks around here
start gathering sparks, diamond flecks,
so by the time I reach

that splayed out, girdled
washing machine
of a train station,

the one whose sky
isn't azured and studded
with constellations, I know

I'm in your orbit,
reading Whitman off the walls,

pondering what particular
hell you've been served
in your cube today,

two blocks west and down
a mile. I've grazed you now,
mouthed you with my

rueful, gap-toothed smile.
And the thought, as I take my seat,
of your swimmer's legs

loose-moving through crowds
for a sandwich

lasts me the whole ride out,
electrons greasing the electric tracks,
until, like the Pulaski Skyway,

I can throw my arm across
your rivers.

THE GOOD NEWS

Mornings now she leaves the house
dressed warmly, crosses two bridges,

counts red-winged blackbirds.
So far a good time, and not even plastic

cup lids nor plastic shit bags ruffling
in the brush along the river

can divert her. Around which bend,
beyond which blaze of forsythia

will the next sorrow appear,
shocking and gawky as a Great Blue?

When she sits down for breakfast,
the names of species that flash

across the window come back to her:
Vireo. Chickadee. She eats her oatmeal,

starts late. No one's employee or child,
she sits unsupervised, impervious,

in a room illuminating manuscripts.
Today it is a lowercase "e" she spends an hour

glazing with gold leaf, and under its dome
a tiny annunciation, with a Mary and a Joseph

she is capable of, and a bearded angel
like a kind uncle bearing the good news,

though she has no idea what the "e"
stands for, or what chapter it might begin.

ENDING THE POEM

Never on light or love.
Never, I'm told, on one of those
Poetry words like keening or wept.
Tears of any kind, in fact,
Are out, and even a rueful
Smile reads smug in the last line.
No small animals, or small
Hands, or anything especially
Beneficent. Don't even think about
Children or old people. Or teenagers,
Lest they drive the poem
Into a ditch two blocks from home.
Nothing delicious nor bitter.
Forget kisses and comeuppance,
As easily as you forget umbrellas
At parties; it's not worth going back.
Don't get moral. Nothing's black
Or white in the end. Never
On silence. Or birdsong. Ever.
And the silence that utterly shadows
The yard at the end of birdsong?
I doubt it. Don't be certain, we ask,
About anything. Ask a question,
Leave a crumb, chase the tail
Of something down a black hole.
Just don't make it black.
Make it that color at the throats
Of poppies, a kind of blue gray black
Like crushed velvet. And feel it
Going down.

ALL SOULS DAY

I was fifty before I really
considered teeth.

At the Advanced Dental Clinic
on Prospect, silver pockets of molars from childhood
are removed, newly enameled.
Everybody Loves Raymond floats on the set,
engrossing as an accident.

How appealing they feel
when she applies the fluoride, pasty and dry,
after the deep cleaning. When I leave,
my smile is sincere, rooted.

Outside, the ginkgo leaves lose their grip
and fall. Through a window,
a film of yellowing ivy,
a woman reads the newspaper in her kitchen, coffee.

Nine months and no one
has visited my father. The teeth are still there, but not the body.
Not a headstone, but a pillow of leaves.

GOLDFINCH, AS HEARD IN EARLY SPRING

Look at my brights,
my yellows—

Watch how fast, how near
impossible to follow

with your eye into branches.
Look at my eye.

All these moral dilemmas.
Laura next door weeping,
a glass of wine on the table—

Who wouldn't place
her thumb on my breast,

if she could? On my sternum.
How fast the heart race
underneath. How dry the mouth.

Who with these powers
needs anything
but water and seed head and sun?

ACKNOWLEDGMENTS

The author would like to thank the editors of the following publications, in which some of the poems here first appeared or are forthcoming:

America Magazine: "Knights of Columbus"
New Ohio Review: "Ending the Poem"
Nytimes.com: "Eden"
2 Bridges Review: "In Manhattan, We Don't Meet for Lunch"
upstreet: "I Fight with Marie, Who Is Five" and "Rainy Day Women"

Abundant thanks to my family of readers and writers, Sally Bliumis-Dunn, Alison Jarvis, Judy Katz, Frances Richey, and June Stein. I am especially grateful to Frances Richey for her insights on ordering the poems here, and to Jessica Greenbaum for her support and inspiration. Deepest thanks and love to Gregory Fagan, my first reader and best friend, and to my siblings, late parents, and children who have given me so many stories to mine. Thank you to Joy Yagid for capturing my town, and me, and to Glenn Wright for his elegant cover design. Finally, to my teachers, Vijay Seshadri and Michael Lally, who always light the way.

Theresa Burns' poetry, reviews, and nonfiction have appeared in *The New York Times, Prairie Schooner, Bellevue Literary Review, America Magazine, The Women's Review of Books, New Ohio Review,* and *upstreet*, among other publications. A long-time book editor in New York and Boston, she holds an MFA in poetry from Sarah Lawrence College. She has taught writing at Seton Hall University, The Fashion Institute of Technology, and the 92nd Street Y.

www.ingramcontent.com/pod-product-compliance
Lightning Source LLC
LaVergne TN
LVHW021123080426
835510LV00021B/3297